What Others Say...

*The best way to describe Dr. Tammy Heflebower would be **transformational**. No one is immune to her incredible wisdom and no one leaves a meeting with her without first searching their soul and being resolute in changing their own behaviors and practices to reach higher levels of expertise.*
She truly inspires others in transformative ways.
> *Dr. Shelley Sweat, President & CEO, The Priddy Foundation*

I attended your "Powerful Presentations" workshop in Denver. Your suggestions and tips made a huge difference and we had our most positive feedback in 5 years! Thank you so much for sharing your "tips of the trade".
> *Sam Fritz, music teacher, Center Grove Public Schools*

I LOVED watching you work. You really brought your 'A' game! I look forward to working with you in the future.
> *Ramiro S. Reyes, Ed.D., Educational Administrator, Assessment & Accountability, Monterey County Office of Education*

What Others Say…

I appreciate your expertise and your input on the evaluation side of things over a year ago, it helped us to move in the right direction for sure. You probably don't hear it enough – but your educational leadership is outstanding!!

> *Melanie J. Mueller, Ed.D. Director of Research, Assessment and Evaluation, Papillion LaVista Community Schools*

Presenting Perfected: Dynamic Delivery

Dynamic

Delivery

This is the second resource in the *Presenting Perfected* series: Everyday solutions for perfecting your presentations.

Dr. Tammy Heflebower

Dedication

To mom and my late dad. Thank you for helping me learn to use my voice to share hope, and to express my passion. You taught me the value of hard work, perseverance, devotion, and the gift of gab! Your sacrifices, support, and unending love pushed me beyond what I thought possible. I am forever grateful. To my brother, Doug. Although our age difference and dissimilar pathways, we've always found our commonalities. Your honesty, grit, and unending support modeled a friendship beyond family. As we've grown, it's been great to rekindle our sibling love and admiration. Thanks for who you are!

Table of Contents:

Part III: Deliver Your Message

Introduction

It is January. I have been in my role as an author and trainer for three months, and I've been asked to conduct my first keynote presentation. The location--Montréal, where French is the primary language. Not only did I need to learn about a new system, but also their existing approach to my controversial topic. I stood behind a podium—stiff and stern, I had memorized my keynote. I used limited inflection, my pacing was too fast, and I had to pause for the information to be interpreted and understood. The topic was a philosophical shift for the audience. There was no physical space for interactivity, so I aborted such infused experiences. Finally…it was over! I survived. The audience was polite, yet I knew my time with them certainly was not a home run. It was maybe a dive into first base, after a struggled at bat. Afterward, I reflected. I learned. I revised. I committed to getting better, much better.

Selling your ideas is grueling! Whether it is being done to a board, a team, your staff, during a teleconference, or an informal gathering--conveying and selling a poignant, memorable message takes specific knowledge and skills. Do you know them? Do you have them? If you are interested in capitalizing your skills as a keynote speaker, CEO, sales manager, coach, or anyone seeking to enhance your presentation and facilitation skills, this book series is for you!

This resource is the second in a series about perfecting your presentations. It culminates key learnings over the course of two decades of full-time public speaking. These included training and speaking engagements both nationally and internationally to local, state, and national boards, administrators, parents, teachers, and business constituents. Each book exemplifies focus on a particular element of making a successful presentation, and the many derivatives of it, from planning through reflection—appetizer through dessert, so-to-speak.

Throughout this specific resource you will learn about how to *deliver* a quality message. Part I describes important considerations for setting the stage—room arrangement, use of sound, managing the audience, and centering yourself. Thoughtful planning suggestions help novice and expert presenters reflect about everything surrounding you and your messaging. Part II embodies essential elements for three types of introductions: informal, formal, and topic-based, as well as important culminating conclusions. Part III focuses on the plethora of considerations for a dynamic delivery of your message. Some ideas noted are getting your group's attention, using your voice effectively, presenter behaviors, engagement, visual enhancements, webinars, facilitation, and the all-important speaker's toolkit. I hope this series will assist you in your planning, preparation, delivery, professionalism, and reflection. Go be great!

I try to create an environment where, when we step onto the set, we're all in character.

Vin Diesel

Part 1: Setting the Stage

Preparation and Outcomes

Prepare your setting for success by ensuring your training or speaking room and arrangement will complement your message. Think of it like prepping a painting surface prior to painting a room, setting a table for a big meal, or sowing soil for planting—excellent preparation prevents pitfalls. In this section, I highlight topics for consideration to include the room arrangement, use of sound, audience management, and your own self-grounding and preparation.

Arrange the Room

The arrangement of your room is paramount. Be certain you have spoken about this during your planning call or meeting with your hiring agency. You want to be certain that the room is arranged to maximize the training experience. There are dozens of arrangement suggestions. Below I detail a few common types with a corresponding characteristics and rationale.

The U Shape:

The U shape is great for groups of 10-20 people. It allows for everyone to easily see and hear one another. This format works well for small group trainings or facilitated sessions, team meetings, retreats, and board meetings. It allows for a presenter or facilitator to be positioned at the open portion of the U, and participants comfortably seated around the outside of the tables making it up. The U format allows for much interspersed dialogue. One cautionary note, be certain participants are not seated near the table legs, with plenty of personal space in between one another.

The Arrow:

This arrangement is likely the most common and my personal preference. It can be used with both large (a few hundred) and small groups (20-50). In this formation, the presenter is placed at the front and center of the room, with rectangular tables angled at an arrow pointing toward the front and center. In this arrangement, all participants can see quite well, and no one is seated with his/her back toward the presenter. Positioned tables closer to the front will need a stronger angle, and those in the middle of the room will be perpendicular to the presenter. Be certain the tables are wide-enough to allow participants to spread out and converse. Thin tables may need to be doubled in order for the personal space to be adequate.

The Rounds:

Using round tables with seats around the back side of them works for groups of up to 100-200, and it easily enables conversations among participants. This format allows for grouping people more easily, and visually insinuates collaboration. If possible, only seat participants in a C formation around the backside of the round table. This way, there is an open space at the area of the round where no chairs are located. The best-case scenario is to refrain from having anyone with their backs toward the presenter. If there are chairs all around, physically turn those chairs facing toward the table so they are now facing the presenter.

The Auditorium

Auditorium seating works for hundreds to thousands of attendees. The format consists of fixed seats in rows with small or no table attachments. Sometimes there is a balcony, often times not. The purpose is solely for participants to listen--signifying a "sit and get" perspective. In fact, in auditorium seating, it is difficult, yet not impossible, to interact effectively. Use paired discussions or standing, paired discussions to add some interaction. One advantage to this setting is that acoustics and technology tend to be high quality. However, this format is the least favorite for any training lasting longer than an hour.

The Conference Breakout

This seating is often of slim tables in long rows with chairs facing forward. Typically this is used from 50-100 people in a tight space—think hotel breakout rooms. It is sometimes referenced as "classroom" style. It allows for limited participation and most focus to be toward the presenter at the front of the room.

Whatever the initial set up, be certain you make it fit what your presentation needs will be. In other words, if you need to angle the tables or move chairs so no backs will be toward you, by all means, do it. The arrangement will immediately suggest and even dictate your interaction capabilities. If you don't like the arrangement, get there early, and move it to best meet your needs. I can't emphasize this enough---if participants cannot easily group, they won't do it. You will lose the effect of your presentation if the arrangement impedes your work.

When planning room arrangement attend to the following:

- Use comfortable chairs with padding and fabric covers. Have just enough, if not even fewer, chairs set out than you might need. You want a room to feel full. Empty chairs create black holes for energy deprivation. Have additional chairs and tables on hand to easily add for overflow. It's better to add than to subtract.

- Allow for appropriate spacing among adults — minimally 12 inches between seats, allowing 18-24 inches for each person seated. They need space for personal items and movement. Note, this is not typically how room arrangers place chairs, so you will need to specifically request this amount of personal space for your participants ahead of time.

- Ensure that room arrangement coincides with the type of training, activities, and physical movement planned. If you expect the entire group to move, is there a large-enough space designated for that? However, be flexible. You may have to modify your delivery to manage a difficult room set up. No matter how much you plan, you will sometimes have to adjust on-the-fly.

- Use tables if participants will need to use additional materials (handouts, sticky notes, highlighters). Ask for such items to be in containers on the tables.

- No matter the table type, arrange them with pathways and walkways so you, and your audience members can easily maneuver the room. Walk in and among the chairs as you are testing your audio equipment to ensure you have the space you will need to move effectively.

Monitor Sound

As mentioned in the first book series (Heflebower, 2018), the sound in the room is important. If participants enter a silent room, it feels empty and stark. You want the room to look and sound inviting. Play upbeat music at a level to be noticeable, yet not so loud that you can still greet participants without shouting.

Use Music

When selecting music, consider what we have learned about our brains. Music is one of the best condition changers. As Rich Allen reminded us, "At the very least, music can enhance motivation, attentions, and feelings of vigor" (p. 113). When you want an audience to be calm and relaxed play music that matches the resting heart rate at 60-80 beats per minute (bpm). Rather, if you want the audience to be energetic and upbeat, play music that is twice that—roughly 120-130 bpm. One way to determine this is to find the beat of the music and count it for six seconds, then multiply that by ten (to total 60 seconds) in order to find out how many bpm the song selection comprises in one minute. Then, create various playlists to match the states you want your audiences to emulate. I have playlists for opening music, closing music, reflection, lunch, and breaks. Use music for transitions, or even a specific call-back song cuing participants to return from an activity or break (Allen, 2008). Be mindful of variations in music appreciation. I tend to use well-known types of popular songs right before I formally begin. For instance, I have used *I'm so excited* by The Pointer Sisters just prior to conducting my training, and *Who let the dogs out?* By Baha Men to close a training. This one adds some humor and the lyrical puns are intentional. Be certain you abide by copyright laws and be sure you are appropriately obtaining your music.

Use of Microphones

When in doubt, use a microphone. In the first book of this series (Heflebower, 2018, p. 32), I discussed the importance of using a microphone, and when it makes most sense to do so. Here, I'll detail the effective use of them.

Address microphone needs prior to your delivery. Do you prefer a handheld, a lapel, or an over-the-ear microphone? If you aren't sure, test out the options. If you do not use many visuals and consequently need a handheld clicker, a handheld mic might work well. Many lapel microphones allow for your hands to be free. This is key if you use a lot of gestures and movement. Yet, lapel microphones work best when attached to a tie or lapel collar, and with someone who has limited head movement. This does not always work as well for what women wear and with the tonality of our voices. As our heads move, we can easily lose sound. Speaking of such, ladies, be mindful that what you wear will allow for the type of microphone you will have at the site. A dress without a belt can be disastrous, because you may have no obvious place to clip the microphone pack. If you end up having to hide the it, that can be uncomfortable and unsightly. Holding a microphone pack in one hand while speaking, looks unprofessional. Consider an over-the-ear microphone connecting system. They produce high quality sound and they come with an assortment of attachments that fit various microphone packs. Using your own system will make you not only feel more comfortable, but will also portray professionalism.

Test the microphone early, prior to too many participants in the room. Be mindful, as the room fills with people the sound will be absorbed, which changes the volume needs considerably. Keep technicians available for slight tweaks just before, and after, you begin. Ensure you have the sound loud enough to easily project your voice at various emphasis levels. Say phrases you will use in your presentation, and annunciate normally. Ensure the sound is rich, not tinny or echoing. Often you will need to adjust the gain levels on the microphone pack in order to enhance the quality of the sound.

Master microphone control. That means, be certain you remember to turn your microphone *on* when speaking to the group, but *off* when you are not. You don't want your microphone on when your audience is engaged in table conversations or when individuals are asking you a question not intended to be heard by the entire room. We are all aware of authentic presenter experiences when the mic was left on as the presenter cleared his/her throat, coughed, or yes—used the restroom. Ahem…manage that mic! Novice presenters often forget to turn on and off buttons, as they are nervous and bombarded with all the many other details. Practice shutting the mic on and off a number of times. Get a feel for the lag time it takes for the sound of your voice to amplify into the room, as well as how the button feels. If you place the mic pack in your pocket or on the backside of your body where you cannot see it, determine and remember the on/off button positions. Each pack varies noticeably. Some are push on/off, some have a switch, still others require you to hold it down for a bit of time. I might also suggest not allowing a technician to turn your mic on and off for you throughout the presentation. Although it is a thoughtful gesture, notoriously they will get distracted and forget, or they simply will not know your mic on and off preferences. Never rely on someone else. As rudimentary as this seems, managing your microphone and the sound of your voice is the sign of an experienced speaker.

Manage Your Audience

Help your audience be respectful of time throughout your presentation. When you take breaks, it is important to get your audience back in their seats and attentive when you need them back. Your actions help the audience manage their responses.

Imbed Timers & Countdowns

Consider using timers and countdowns. These help your audience better mind the timeframes for breaks and lunch, and most assuredly get you started on time. Few things are more distracting than when the emcee or presenter is haphazardly trying to get the group's attention to start. There are oodles of electronic timers you can find online. I also like having countdowns imbedded into my presentation, so as to keep me from toggling back and forth between or among software programs as the presentation is underway.

Begin on Time; End Early

It likely goes without much discussion, yet start on time. You immediately send a message about expectations when you honor the time of those who are prompt. If, for some unforeseen reason, you must start a bit late, be certain you announce it. Begin by verbally honoring those there on time by sharing your appreciation, and that you will begin in five minutes.

As important as beginning on time is, ending a bit early is also essential. Yes, you heard that right—early. Five minutes early is completely acceptable and allows for your host to wrap up with necessary announcements. Never, ever go over your allotted time. Never. It's a sign of disrespect and lack of planning.

Prepare a Filler (Just in Case!)

Create set of filler options you can use as needed. This might include a few additional slides, a story, or an activity that could be used to close a gap of remaining or "dead" time. Think of this similar to a riff that musicians use when doing improvisation. They are given reign to expend time creating and grooving a solo. This is a presenter riff. Use them as needed to uplift energy, provide active participation, or change the audience state. Often in all day training situations, there is five to ten minutes before a scheduled break or lunch, where a planned riff is warranted. I often have a related set of slides and an activity that allows for me to extend 15-20 minutes, if needed. Many times you will not need them. Yet, prepare them and know which topic-related riffs you will imbed.

Center Yourself

You are about to do something most fear—present to adults. Don't take that lightly. It's difficult. In fact, it's downright frightening for most, and debilitating for many. Find a way to center yourself prior to entering the presentation location. It might be a few minutes in your car, backstage, or even in the restroom. Wherever you can take a few deep breaths, capture a calming moment, or give yourself a bit of positive self-talk, find the time and do it.

That moment of calm will help you deal with the plethora of frazzled frenzy you may encounter as you arrive. There will be people to meet, hands to shake, set up to complete, and unanticipated problems to solve on the spot. Be certain you've lowered your anxiety with a calming practice before you enter into your location.

Not only is important to calm yourself, but hydrate before, during, and after. Water is the drink of choice while presenting. Although you may crave other drinks (those can come later!), caffeinated drinks paired with unexpected nerves may make you jittery and tense. Carbonated beverages paired with a microphone can be embarrassing. Think inadvertent belching or hiccupping, here. Water. Good, old-fashioned water, is best. Some presenters refrain from taking in fluids, as they worry about needing to use the restroom too often. Actually, your body will crave the hydration and adjust (in most instances). Bring your own water, and plenty of it, in the container you favor. Never rely on someone else to provide something as essential to your presentation, as water. It will help you perform optimally.

Throughout this portion of the resource, I highlighted the significance of setting the stage for a great presentation—from room arrangement and use of sound, to managing both your audience and yourself. The next part of this resource details the components of effective introductions.

We don't know where our first impressions come from or precisely what they mean, so we don't always appreciate their fragility.

Malcolm Gladwell

Part 2:

Effective Introductions & Conclusions

Introductions and conclusions matter. Introducing yourself and introducing your topic are both challenging, yet one of the most important things we do. Closing effectively is equally as demanding. In this segment, we will explore your informal and formal personal introductions first. Later, we will discuss ways to introduce your topic and culminate your closing.

A great introduction is well-planned and it gives you a

chance to do the following (Karia, 2012):

- Build connections with your audience;

- Create a first impression that will determine your audience's receptiveness towards you and your message;

- Set the tone for your time together;

- Grab the audience's attention within the first 30 seconds so they don't mentally check out; and

- Put you a bit at ease to relax and obtain confidence with the group.

A realization in quality presenting is that it is one thing to be a recognized communicator and presenter with your local work team, another to be strong in a company, then harder to be a strong presenter at the regional or statewide level, and the hardest to do so at the national and international level. The reason is simple—

relationships. When you have relationships with your audience, they cut you slack and they are more understanding because they know you. However, in many presenting gigs—at least the first time—they are done with an unknown audience in an unknown place. You begin your relationship building through an effective introduction.

Informal Introductions: What *to* Do

Whether you like it or not, you are *on* from the minute audience members first see you, until you are far gone from the parking lot. Therefore, a few tricks of the trade will help.

Arrive first. You must be there before your audience arrives to ensure everything is ready--the room arrangement, technology set-up, sound, print resources, and temperature are all perfect. As audience members arrive you are in the informal greeting mode. This requires you to personally greet each participant you can. The following considerations will make you more successful when thinking about your informal introduction techniques.

Smile. This seems trite, yet remember, you will be thinking about a dozen other things, and those concerns and stresses will likely show on your face. Practice your smile. Yep. Practice it. It should be genuine.

Touch, if possible. In some way, offer appropriate touch as you informally introduce yourself to your participants. There is truly something magical about it. The handshake is still the most common form of touch. Be sure your handshake is strong, single-handed, yet not overpowering. Ladies, you *must* have a strong handshake. No mush hand, no "pinch-like" handshake. Look each person in the eye, shake his/her hand for about two seconds (longer gets competitive, shorter is awkward), while welcoming and introducing yourself. Share a verbal welcome and an informal introduction to each person you possibly can. I elect to use my first name only, as both my names together are a mouthful. I also think it sends a more informal and conversational style. You may even find yourself going from table to table to do so. Say something as basic as, "Welcome. Thanks for coming." "Hello. Glad you are here!" Get (and remember) names. Say the person's name back to them. Use a few of the group members' names as you are in your first half hour of time together. These incidental and informal introductions immediately connect your audience members to you. It sends a clear message that you are personable, relatable, and you sincerely care about them taking the time to be with you.

Formal Introductions: What _To_ Do

There are a variety of effective ways to craft a formal introduction of yourself to the group. The following are a few suggestions for consideration (Pike, 1989, Karia, 2012; DiResta, 2017). Select one or a couple you can merge together about which you will master and repeat easily.

1. Begin with a unique story. They are personal and connect your audience to you immediately. They can help you create a mind metaphor and will help your audience see you in a "human" light. Ensure your story is, in fact, yours. What story is signature to you? Do you play an unusual instrument? Are you a baseball or soccer mom? Do you live in a unique area of the country? What makes you different from others presenting on the topic or during the conference? When you think about those differences, you will forge your signature story. Then, enhance it. Make it come to life through the senses. What did something smell like? How did something feel? Get some emotion (hopefully, joyous) into the room.

2. Craft a catchy phrase—"a phrase, that pays" as some say (Gordon, 2011). This memorable phrase may serve as an anchor for the rest of your presentation, upon which you will build your key points. Consider some you know and recognize: "Just do it!", "A kiss begins with Kay", "You can do it, we can help". These offer a creative way to capture attention and introduce your topic.

3. Use a thoughtful set of questions to get your audience thinking and wondering. "Who is your favorite leader? What makes him or her great?" This example immediately gets your audience focused on something of relevance you will connect to the topic. It also frames the topic in a positive way.

4. Help the audience identify a problem. What is a problem the audience is likely experiencing at that moment? Name it. Begin by stating it. "Put words in

their mouths"—"I'm sure you were hoping for a blizzard." "I bet you have more stress than most other occupations." "Selling a product so difficult these days." By identifying a problem, quickly followed by the promise of a solution or ideas to help, you will pique the interest of your participants.

5. Share a powerful quote as another effective way to begin or enhance your introduction. A quote can "say" just the right thing, without you actually saying it. It helps you identify a feeling, a need, or a concern within the audience—all the while deflecting the genesis away from you. In other words, it can put a topic into the room without it being personalized to you. For example, Thomas Edison's famous quote, "Genius is one percent inspiration and ninety-nine percent perspiration" may be a great way to open a discussion about effort and hard work. You might

consider a different quote for a topic on planning an important message, like Effie Jones' famous quote, "Failing to plan is a plan to fail." The quotes focus your message and are exemplified by others' words. Consider them as a connector for your audience.

6. Utilize an interesting fact or figure as yet another way to grab your audience's attention. "What is the number one concern for leaders?" "Why do most people hate their jobs?" Why are we such an advanced country, yet still have such issues with poverty and homelessness?" These are examples of questions that connect you to your topic, and make the audience begin actively thinking.

7. Reference something notable that just happened prior to you speaking (Karia, 2012). Did you notice the exorbitant number of round-a-bouts on the way to the training? Did something silly occur in your hotel

(that is appropriate to share)? Did the downpour everyone just experienced cause a particularly interesting situation for you? That reference now can also become a mini, appropriate and personalized story.

8. Begin with something really unique about where you are speaking or the topic at hand. Is your location the smallest in the area, so there is no stoplight? Does the location have a unique fact about which most, if not all, would relate to? Is there a favorite sports team competing in a big game? Learn about the area, as it always helps audiences to appreciate the effort you took to know about them better.

It is not enough to consider the approach to your formal introduction. You must carefully plan it, practice it, and deliver it. Do so, repeatedly. You want your words to flow, your timing to be perfect, and your formal introduction to really grab the attention of your audience. Your introduction sets the tone for the rest of your time with the group. Make it strong. Make it great!

Begin planning your introduction carefully by using an effective attention grabber you created, or consider one of the ideas mentioned previously. Write it out. Yes. Stop right now, and write it out. You can begin with key concepts — maybe even jotted on sticky notes. Yet, build it into sentences and paragraphs. This is important!

Next, read every word aloud, carefully. Read it again. Do you have the perfect phrasing? Do you catch yourself stumbling over a few words? If need be, change them. If you stumble now, it is likely you will do so later in front of your audience. A great rule of thumb is to have a maximum of 10-12 words in any one sentence (Gordon, 2011). The rationale is simple. Your audience listens in chunks. If your phrases are too long, your audience gets lost in wordiness.

Go back to your introduction and count the words you have per sentence. Be sure that your sentences vary in length, and there are thoughtful transitions between any key points.

Formal Introductions: What _Not_ to Do

Introductions can, and often do, fall very flat. That first experience with your audience may exhibit some of the negative behaviors we noted previously. Guard against these characteristics of _ineffective_ introductions.

1. A "me-focused"(Karia, 2012) introduction—no one wants to hear your entire biography— no one! When a speaker makes the first few minutes (or more) all about forcing the audience to listen to them and their plethora of accomplishments, it feels self-centered and stuffy. You do not want your first few minutes to leave an audience wondering who the training is really for and about, anyway. Is it simply a chance

for you to hear yourself talk about you? Or, is it really going to be more about connecting with your audience in an authentic way, in order to foster listening ears and an open mind? An audience can "smell out" your insincerity and you will have lost them before you actually begin.

2. Another downfall is opening with the obligatory gratitude, "Thank you, (host). My name is _____. I am so happy to be with you. I'd like to introduce myself" (Karia, 2012). This introduction feels obligatory to your audience, so get their attention, then share gratitude to your host or hosting organization a bit later. As Karia (2012) said, "Unfortunately, most presentations today have very boring, predictable openings that turn audience members off…" (p. 21-22).

3. Do not allow the introduction of yourself to get too long. Keep it focused and relatively short—no more than a few minutes. In fact, two-three minutes is probably plenty. Audiences need to know enough about you to listen, yet not so much they lose interest.

4. Yet another "what not to do" is the attempt at opening with a joke (Karia, 2012). This type of introduction can miss the mark on so many levels. First, most people are lousy joke-tellers. Without clearly knowing your audience and the invisible boundaries of appropriateness, most jokes will lack the luster they were hoped to surface. Remember, your audience did not sign up for a comedy club routine, they expect you to be professional, knowledgeable, and engaging. A joke will virtually always offend someone in the room—that is what

makes them funny. Yet, this is not what your audience came to hear. Instead, jokes detract from your message. They are not worth the risk.

Introducing Your Topic and Processes:

As important as your informal and formal introductions of yourself are, equally important is the way you introduce the topic at hand. Some presenters may merge this into the formal introduction of themselves, yet others will transition from their own information to the theme. Whichever, be deliberate and make that transition smoothly.

Introducing the Topic

Introduce the topic both inductively and deductively. In other words, be sure to provide enough of the big picture to give those who need to see it, a map of where this is headed. Additionally, share the specific goals and objectives you will address somewhere within the introduction to the matter. Both big picture and specific components are important.

Introducing the Processes

Plan for purposeful group interaction. Group participants and explain those processes. Will you want the audience to interact with one another? How? Decide that ahead of time, and infuse these groupings as part of the way in which you'll provide reflection about the subject matter. You are essentially introducing how they will have voice and opportunities for participation. Will you use small partner groups, table teams, large group interactions? Name the groups and provide a visual cue that will help them know what to do when they see it. Consistently reference the groups—don't call them a shoulder partner one minute and a seatmate the next. It is important to note that groupings should be natural and relatively easy to configure.

Consider adding a visual icon on any slides for each

grouping or discussion reflection opportunity. For instance, use a picture of a team for the table team conversation; use a picture of a partner group for the elbow or shoulder partner conversation; apply a solo thinker for the time you want your audience to simply pause and reflect independently. These pictures or icons will connect your processes for discourse with the content delivery. It creates a flow between presenting and audience deliberation.

Openers

A great way to introduce the groupings as well as the content is to have each group of participants discuss or explore an opener or "teaser" to the presentation content. Openers are operational energizers. Done a bit subtly, adult audiences respond with surprise and appreciation. You want your audience to feel that something will be different from the typical, lack-luster meetings they attend. They often reduce tension and anxieties, add a bit of energy into the room, and set a tone for involvement. If you are speaking about leadership, ask your table team to first introduce themselves, and then discuss the qualities of great leaders they know. This way, you are getting your audience to know one another, all they while warming up their brains around the topic at hand. You might consider others like "Stump your team" where you tell them a couple of things, one that isn't true of you, and they must decide which that is. Another might simply be finding something a small group has in common that starts with the same letter of the alphabet. For instance, maybe everyone agrees they all like pizza. Although they can sometimes feel a bit silly at first, they invite your audience to get their own voices into the room in a positive manner. When that happens, a remarkable byproduct occurs—you feel more comfortable and relaxed. There are a variety of suggestions and resources (Solem & Pike, 1997; Jensen, 1998; Cross, 2009;

Duarte, 2012).

Use Schedules and Norms of Operation

Humans work more efficiently and effectively when there are reasonable, adult-centered schedules and boundaries. Everyone wants to know how the day will play out, as most are managing a myriad of responsibilities outside of your training. By sharing a schedule, your audience can anticipate breaks, lunch, and ending times, in order to monitor times throughout the day they can check devices and their other obligations. Simply by doing so, you respect them and their time.

Use a limited set of "norms" about which your audience can abide. These are a small number of operational procedures to include things like how and when to ask questions, your requests for participation, and simple kindness toward one another. These might include, but are not limited to:

- Please abide by the attention signal.

- Take care of your personal needs.

- Monitor your time at breaks and lunch.

- Please limit your technology use to breaks.

- Enjoy your day!

Employ succinct, yet a kind (maybe even a humorous) approach to delivering them. I find that by doing this up front, you mitigate possible issues later on.

Conclude Emphatically

Just as openers infuse early energy into the room, closers tie things together. A good closer helps you revisit the key content and helps your audience leave with actions. Participants might practice what they learned, create a plan for using the information in the near future, or share a key learning. Often, they function as a celebration of your time together and formally close your training session.

Plan your ending virtually as much as you plan your introduction. An encapsulating quote, a perfect imbedded video, or simply a heartfelt story can perfectly end an effective presentation. It doesn't need to be long—three to five minutes. Be certain it culminates the learning and leaves your audience inspired. As with opening ideas, there are also great print and web resources dedicated to closings in some of the same of the materials and authors listed above.

Review the Message Format

You likely recall the message format shared in the first book series. A brief summary follows (Heflebower, 2018, p. 19):

- Identify the purpose and outcomes of the presentation clearly and at early stages. This can and should be infused into the introduction of your topic without it feeling mechanical or obligatory.

- Consider using an opener to cultivate relationships within your audience and with you. Openers are described a bit more below.

- Develop key ideas early. Your audience needs have a significant "take-away" within the first hour. This also creates and easy win, for you.

- Use and organize appropriate materials to support your message. Reference your materials regularly.

- Use meaningful, purposeful, and engaging activities and interactive learning strategies. Intersperse them thoughtfully — about every 20-30 minutes.

- Check for audience understanding and input on a regular basis; provide a means for adults to ask questions in a public and/or private manner. Will you use a parking lot format or allow for questions from the floor?

- Allow time for audience application and reflection. Consider an activity or action plan to help them leave with something tangible.

- Provide adequate closure and effective summary of your key points.

Ensuring your message is thoughtfully organized helps your audience make sense of it and remember it. Review your message and format the morning of your delivery, *no matter how many times you have previously delivered it.* Remember, you have done thousands of things in between times. Your brain will thank you for the preparation. Words will flow more naturally, and your confidence will increase.

In this section, I explored the importance of your three introduction types and summarizing conclusion. The next part of this resource details the components of a dynamic delivery.

The human brain is a wonderful organ. It starts to work as soon as you are born and doesn't stop until you get up to deliver a speech.
George Jessel

Part 3:

Deliver Your Message

Delivery Considerations

You've planned your message, aligned it to the intended outcomes, and set the physical stage. It is now time to dynamically deliver your message. In this chapter, I will highlight the components of getting your group's attention, using your voice effectively, and engaging with your participants.

Get the Group's Attention

Get your group's full attention before you speak. Hands down, this is SO important! Do not speak to a group without them attending to you. Getting attention prior to speaking does a couple of key things. One is quite obvious—it allows all to hear your information, and likely saves twenty individual questions, later. Yet a more implicit reason is that it sends a subtle message that you are in control of the room. Audiences actually want to be assured of that. They need to know that someone in the room is in control. They may not outwardly tell you they need it, but they need to know they are safe—respectful behaviors are expected and monitored, and that someone in the space is the leader. Consider using a phrase like, "May I ask you to rejoin us." Or, "Please pause your conversations." Both phrases indicate that you need their attention at this time, and you are kindly asking for it. Yet, it also implies the group doesn't have to completely *stop* what they are doing forever. Instead, they will pause to give you attention, and later can complete conversations. This is important for adult audiences. Remember, what they have to say is important, too. Those collegial phrases subtly honor your participants, while asking them to cease their current conversations.

Speak Well; Be Passionate

Speak intelligently. As you review your planned message, notice how your planned message compares to your delivered one. Be mindful of slang and shortened words, like "yeah, kinda, sorta..." and expunge them from your vocabulary! You don't need to sound like a thesaurus, yet you need a strong command and use of the language.

Share your message passionately. An audience perceives and appreciates presenters who really care about their topic. Your use of inflection and word choice highlight that passion. Nevertheless, A speaker who is overly energetic for the entire time, tires an audience. Conversely, a speaker who has limited inflection and inspiration will bore them to death. Write out much of what you want to say, rehearse it regularly, in order to deliver it well.

Use Your Voice Effectively

Your voice is your presentation instrument. Warm it up, use it effectively, and treat it kindly. Pay attention to how you signify emphasis throughout your message. Ensure variation.

Speak Clearly and Powerfully

Voice dramatically affects audiences. Listen to your voice. Begin by simply standing and delivering your introduction. Is your voice rich and formidable? Is it too forceful and loud? Is it too highly pitched? Our voices naturally raise as we get nervous, and in some cases will raise an octave. A high-pitched, shrill voice in a microphone can be nails on a chalkboard. A hurdle your audience will not be able jump. Practice. Ensuring your breathing is deep and filling up your lungs—more diaphragmatic. This naturally enhances your pitch and allows your voice to be powerful in all ranges. A good strategy is to hold out your finger one foot in front of your mouth. Then pretend you are blowing out a candle. That feeling and that breath intensity is the one you want to use while presenting. Attend to relaxing your shoulders and throat, straightening your posture, and breathing deeply as you begin (Hilary Blair, CONSA conference November 1, 2018). If you haven't, read about or even get voice coaching from a trained speech therapist or pathologist. You will learn great warm-up strategies, pitch perfection, and the importance of using your voice without straining it. Does your voice get easily strained? If your voice feels tired or sounds hoarse, afterward you may need support in using your voice more appropriately. Be mindful that your vocal folds need rest after much use. If you speak all day, then exert your voice to speak with clients over a loud restaurant at dinner, your voice will pay an enormous price. Take care of most important tool in your presenter toolbox, your voice. These suggestions seem so straightforward, and yet so many speakers never really hear to themselves speak. Do so.

Annunciate. Articulate without over-emphasizing. Some presenters over do their consonants. Be careful. You want to be certain you are understood, yet that your voice sounds natural. If you have awkward words or phrases to say, something like "sound specificity" or "Heflebower" be certain you say it aloud many times, articulating and annunciating the words and phrases clearly. Do so in a microphone and practice in a location where it echoes.

Pace Well

Another important use of sound is pacing. You want your words and phrases to flow with ease. The pause is an important component of sound pacing. The pause is powerful in emphasis, in using humor effectively, and in providing thoughtful reflection. It means you must be content with silence. Allow your words to land. Let there be some silence occasionally, as it provides variation and impact. We all know the importance of the pause after a comment intending humor. It takes a few seconds for the audience to hear your words and react. Let that happen. Be mindful that the larger the room and the more the acoustics perpetuate echoing, your pausing will be more often, intentional, and your pacing will need to slow.

Avoid the Dreaded Filler Words

Filler words are the kiss of death. They truly alienate your audience immediately. Why? Because we all remember our required speech class, and the emphasis on deleting filler words from our vocabulary. We expect presenters to refrain from filler words—"um", "uh", "well", "yeah", "like", "so"… Period. These are prevalent in casual conversation, yet simply cannot be part of your professional speaking vocabulary. As Christopher Bell (University of Colorado at Colorado Springs Communications Professor, August 16, 2018) said, during college freshman orientation said, "Nothing intelligent follows three "likes". If you aren't sure about your own speaking habits, ask a friend or colleague. They know. Use a couple of helpful applications called *Um* or *LikeSo*. The apps listen to you speak, count your filler words, and report them. What useful and unobtrusive tools to help you perfect the sound of silence.

You might master this refrain during your formal presentation, yet realize they creep back in when you are taking questions or doing something a bit more off-the-cuff. Remember to listen, pause, think, answer. Confident and competent speakers are comfortable with periods of silence. No filler words are needed. They are simply distracting.

Watch Up-Speak

In addition to unconscious speaking slang, some presenters exercise up-speak (DiResta, 2019). This is the notion of ending many of your sentences in an upward sound. Some even add up-speak terms such as, "Right?" "Make Sense?" "Okay?" All of which lessen your credibility. Instead, end directions or requests in a down-tone—when your voice actually drops in sound. This sounds more authoritative and confident. When raise your voice at the end of the sentence, it makes what you say sound optional or uncertain. Practice this a bit. Say a few words—even your name. Do you naturally end upward or downward? Check yourself, and monitor your up-speak accordingly.

Presenter Behaviors

Presenter behaviors marry with an outstanding message. The two together, are a perfect union. A strong message with limited presenting delivery behaviors leave participants disappointed. Often an audience reveres a well-known author, about whose work they have read for years, attend a session with high hopes, only to leave dissatisfied. The famous writer ineffectively shared his/her work. Conversely, a presenter with strong presenting skills only, leaves an audience feeling hollow if there is not a corresponding, compelling content-related message. Skilled presenters master *both*.

Have Presence

When you walk into a room, what do others think? How do they perceive you? Watch. Notice. These are important considerations worth perceiving. If people turn their heads a bit, give you eye contact, and engage in conversation, you have presence. You want that as a presenter. You should be noticed, and in a positive way.

How do you walk? Videotape yourself in order to observe your movement patterns and tendencies. You want to walk confidently with straight posture, stomach held tight, and leading your gait heal to toe. If you slouch, clomp your feet, or have awkward movement patterns, over half of your audience already judged you accordingly—most likely negatively. Small things matter when you are visually summing up a presenter. In fact, your audience has already formed a tentative opinion about you prior to you ever opening your mouth. They have watched whether or not you have interacted or if you were more stand-off-ish. They notice everything. Your attire, accessories, and thus…your presence. In fact, Michael Solomon, PhD, psychologist, at New York University (2005) coined the phrase "7-11 rule" where he estimated that people make eleven decisions about you within the first seven seconds of meeting that can forever shape the nature of the relationship. Even is your audience made only three decisions about you, make them favorable. If you need support, there are a variety of print and online resources to assist you. One I recommend is titled, *Brilliant body language* by Max Eggert (2010).

Mind Your Attire

Be mindful of your attire and the image it portrays. You can certainly be stylish *and* professional. Gentlemen, read about the types of jackets, shirt collars and ties that enhance your body type. One big mistake gentlemen make is that their clothes do not fit. They may have fit a year ago, or the last time you put on that jacket, yet not now. The shirt might pull and not allow a male presenter to move his arms freely. His pants may be too long or too short, or the tell-tale faux pas—the suit jacket sleeves are too long. If people are going to give up time and often money to see you, care enough to tailor your clothing appropriately. Ladies, pay attention. Pay very close attention to this. This should not serve as your first chance to walk from Vogue magazine. If in doubt, be more conservative in your dress and add more stylish accessories—a fun bracelet, scarf, or pair of shoes. Overdress a bit more than your audience. Ensure your shoes are polished, fashionable, yet practical. Often you are standing or moving on a stage, tile, or low piled carpet floor that may hurt your feet and legs over time. Be certain your attire is professional, fits you well, and is comfortable.

Portray Confidence

Be confident, *not* arrogant. A presenter exuding confidence is poised and knowledgeable. Yet, he or she is considerate and a continual learner in his/her field. Too many presenters teeter into over-confidence, and an audience will perceive that immediately. Arrogant presenters truly convey they are the best, and no one knows as much, or is as good as they. Never let yourself dip into that abyss. You should be assured, self-reliant, and courageous to do this work well. Otherwise, everyone could and would do it. Nevertheless, *refrain emphatically from superiority*. And, remember, perceiving haughtiness is an audience's decision. You may not intend to have such a persona, still if even one audience member senses your arrogance, you have lost. Period. I have watched it ruin otherwise exceptional presenters—those I thought were at the pinnacle in their field, only to listen to audience comments and watch colleagues roll their eyes about another's inflated self-ego. Appreciate positive feedback, but never, never let it go to your head.

Engage me. Don't Irritate Me.

Audiences want to be engaged. Adult audiences don't want to do "childish" activities about which they see no point. For example, don't break into a silly song, expecting me to sing along, if I'm not really into the training. Now, that does not mean that you will be serious and never have some child-like moments, but child-like is different than childish. Instead, use adult-centered activities that will be engaging. Some examples for engagement are included within the following section.

Use humor

Adults appreciate a sense of humor. In fact, it will connect an audience to you and the content faster than most other tactics. Yet, the humor should always be self-deprecating and appropriate. Today's adult humor runs the gamut. Be cautious and realize that "comedy show humor" works with late night crowds who may have imbibed adult beverages. It won't work with professional audiences. One wrong move with humor can derail the entire presentation. Like the familiar idiom spoken by Hungerford (1878), "Beauty is in the eye of the beholder." Well, humor is in the brain of the beholder. It is important to consider the humor you want to insert and try it out first with a few different groups—maybe a dinner party or a small group of friends. Do so when and where if it goes a bit awry or insulting, the audience is small and didn't pay to see you! You may have heard it said, "If in doubt, leave it out." Do not go too far to the fringes in using your humor. A funny story, a set of silly pictures that connect your ideas might be a great place to start. The key to using humor, is understanding and using the power of the pause (Gordon, 2011). Humor needs to land. It needs time and space in the room, to be effective. Sarcasm is but one mode of effective, adult humor. Yet, again, it needs to be used tactfully and not at the expense of others in the room.

Videoclips inserted at the perfect moment can provide an element of humor. In fact, using videos (about which you have obtained permission) often adds humor into the room indirectly. It is a safer way to start. Also, presenters who are not naturally funny, may want to imbed a few humorous quotes or videos. The audience laughter actually settles most presenters and puts them a bit more at ease.

In most cases, humor comes as a risk worth taking. Where a joke during an intro is not, use of humor—at an appropriate point in the presentation, is. Be mindful, an honest attempt to infuse humor is often not only appreciated, but also celebrated by the masses. Yet, a few participants may find it offensive. It is a topic for your reflection. If you find that most people laugh at your humor during conversations, gatherings, and impromptu conversations, you are skilled at infusing humor. If, however, most of your closest friends wouldn't consider you funny, then use it sparingly at first. Add it into places for an effect. Over time, you may find you can introduce it more naturally into the "conversation" of your presentation.

Connect Naturally

Audiences are people. People crave connections. So, a great presenter must connect with audience members—no matter how many are in the room. One way to connect is to ensure you obtain and maintain eye contact with individuals. There used to be an old tactic shared in speech class called look above. In other words, look just above the heads of your audience members in order to stifle nervousness. Yet, everyone in the room notices when the presenter doesn't look at people. It's awkward, plain and simple. So, begin by scanning the first few rows. Allow your eyes to pan the room, pausing at about every fourth or fifth person. As you pause momentarily, look at them. Connect with them. Then, continue that strategy as you gradually move your gaze left, middle, right, front, back, outside edges, inside edges, all over the room. You would hope to look everyone in the eye throughout a session lasting a few hours. Your audience will know and notice.

Visuals & Print Materials

Strong visuals and print materials augment your message. Some presenters go with out either. Others rely heavily on them both. Whichever your message and your style, gravitate toward is what is right for you. Using them meritoriously is key.

Visual Enhancements

Although some presenters (mostly keynoters) are quite successful without using any form of visual support, most aren't. Furthermore, remember that using multiple modalities (auditory, visual, kinesthetic) better cements learning in the brain. As Feinstein (2006) stated, "The visual sense is arguably the most powerful way that the brain gathers information about the environment, and the processing of visual data and its resulting images is intimately and essentially linked to learning and cognition"

(p. 491). In fact, Allen reiterated that point when he concluded, "Maximizing the visual field means attending to the total training environment, including walls, bulletin boards, ceilings, and windows, using props, displays, images, and posters. When we use our entire teaching stage, our training becomes akin to a surround-sound experience, advancing learning to a new level" (p. 106). Therefore, by using well-planned visuals, you can better ensure your audience remembers your message.

Plan Your Message Thoughtfully

As mentioned in the first book of this series, be certain you have considered your audience size, the type of training you are conducting (keynote versus training, for instance), and your content options (Heflebower, 2018, pp. 28-46). That will naturally drive the amount of visual support you will need.

Some presenters suggest brainstorming your key and supporting ideas first by placing one idea on a sticky note. Arranging (and rearranging) those sticky notes helps you first establish your thinking. Often, when you design using presentation software, the linear nature of such software programs — one slide after another--may actually stifle your thinking and planning. Break your big ideas into little ones, and arrange them into a logical order that makes sense to you as the presenter, as well as to the audience. After clearly suggesting your ideas, move them into visual formats.

Presentation Software Tips

One visual format is presentation software. Using it is still a common format for visual support. Although it's been given a bit of a bad rap, recall "Death by power point", such software is designed to enhance presentations. I'm often asked my preferences among those most common options (Google, Power Point, Keynote, and Prezi), and I still use Power Point for a number of reasons. First, you don't have to have internet connectivity for use. Secondly, it is still most common and can more easily be shared with others using either PC or Mac platforms, whereas Keynote requires more steps. Prezi and Google offer some attractive visual options more limited in Power Point. Whatever your preference, get comfortable with your software and learn and use its many features.

As you place your brainstormed ideas onto the slides, remember a few key slide development ideas:

- Put only the main points on a slide. Keep your notes and smaller details in the notes section for your reference.

- Place no more than six lines of text on a slide.

- Use a minimum of 24 pt. font, yet be mindful of the room size. You may need larger font size.

- Bring your slides to life with pictures, not clip art.

- Use only one or two font styles. You don't want to confuse your audience with various fonts.

- Ensure that font style, color and size is an easy read. Look at your slides from afar. Some fonts are more easily noticed than others. Stick with Times or Arial variations if in doubt.

- Be consistent with style, color and letter size.

- Use animation sparingly. Avoid distracting or annoying your audience with sound or transitions that may make audience members motion sick.

- Imbed video and audio clips. Be certain you know where they are coming in your presentation. Some people insert a black screen to signal you, as the presenter, that a video is upcoming. It allows you to set it up and not surprise your audience with an irrelevant clip.

Paying attention to slide design details makes you a more elite presenter.

Review and Review Some More

See your work as a participant. Be certain you review your work a number of times. In fact, someone once told me, review your writing one time for as many people in your audience. Therefore, you would review it fifty times for an audience size of 50 participants. Although that seems excessive, the point is that you cannot review it enough. You will most assuredly find conventional errors in grammar, spelling, capitalization, and the like.

Not only check your work carefully for spelling mistakes and grammatical errors, but also for how your work flows. Think of it like you are learning it for the first time by running through it as a new learner. Additionally, know your work and the order of your slides well enough to be able to present without referencing your software slides. And, refrain from reading the content on your slides. As Karia (2017) stated, "If you and your PowerPoint are saying the same thing, one of you is not needed" (p. 141).

Handout Design

A supportive handout truly strengthens a strong presentation. You want handouts to supplement, not supplant it. If your handout contains everything you are discussing, why would your audience need to listen? Instead, allow your handout to provide active responses to key questions or places for participants to take notes. This helps deepen understanding of your content and presentation ideas.

Add details to help your audience follow along. One important feature is to ensure your handout is paginated. I like to add a picture of the handout slide with the corresponding page to my visual presentation slides. This allows your audience to easily know if there is an equivalent handout page or whether they need to take their own notes. It simply makes following along with a handout easier. Another feature is about where to place your biographical information. If you print a biography, consider adding it at the end of your handout instead of the beginning of it. This makes your audience realize the training isn't about *you*. Also, one more tip is to provide blank notes pages at the back of your handout, as well as any activity sheets they will reference often.

Although this should go without much discussion, be certain you have obtained the rights to share printed, visual, or imbedded video information. If you are in doubt, check the many online sources, like copyright.com to help you. Plan ahead, as your request may take a few days to a few weeks for a response from the author or copyright holder.

Presenting via Webinar

Presentations are done in various environments. A common one today is using some form of webinar software from a remote location. Although this is a great convenience as a presenter, since you aren't having to travel to your site, you do give up the personal factor you obtain onsite. I often encourage presenters to use web formats as a follow-up instrument, rather than a first training opportunity. The In order for a webinar to be successful, internet connectivity at all sites webbing in is critical. Be certain to test this out prior to contracting the webinar, as well as 15-30 minutes prior to the start of the session.

Webinars can be effective and cost-efficient when done properly. Below are a few checks for consideration:

- Check your lighting. Will it stay the same throughout the time? Do you have shadows or glares that might impede the camera?

- Review to ensure shine on face and/or glasses isn't distracting.

- Check your background (pictures, books, etc.)

- Be sure all pets are contained. No one needs to see a cat slithering around desk!

- Account for ancillary sounds (doorbells, air conditioner, heaters, fans, etc.).

- Ensure your computer is secure and the angle stays consistent.

- Attend to your eye and body movements. Is your camera located in a place you will easily look into, or will you be referencing something where your gaze will drift regularly? Will your gestures enhance the presentation and be seen? Will they be cut off?

- Check the sound both directions. Can you easily hear those on the other end? Do you need to use headphones? Would an additional speaker assist? Can you also be heard well on the receiving side?

- Check your comforts. Is the temperature okay? Will your face flush if you close the door and it gets too hot? Do you need water to drink?

- Mute participants not speaking. Any noises will be picked up and will be distracting. Think someone keyboarding—that will be heard!

- Use video as along as it will be seen and heard without delays. It's a good way to add a mode change, yet needs to be considered useful not distracting.

- Be certain you know, and can use, all of the tools in the webinar software platform. Will you take questions? Can you effectively use the chat boxes or questioning options?

Webinars offer a useful follow-up or question and answer platform for attendees. They are less expensive, and can be very helpful in highlighting a specific detail or component of your message. By attending to the aforementioned suggestions it will serve as an additional and effective learning mode.

Facilitation

Another important role often needed when working with adult audiences is that of a facilitator. Hunter (2007) declared: "Facilitation is an improvisatory art within an agreed and negotiated structure" (p. 73). A skilled facilitator helps groups accomplish common goals with synergy and success. "It often involves helping others face difficult, sometimes unobvious, issues with creativity and collaboration" (Heflebower, 2018, pp. 36-37). The end result is to achieve unanimous, win-win types of solutions. Facilitating an audience may last a few hours to one full day at shortest, and multiple days or a series of intermittent days to accomplish longer-term goals.

Experienced facilitators master the art of questioning—knowing what types of questions to ask and when. They elicit open-ended responses that enable stronger collective dialogue, perspective analysis, and inclusiveness of the group participants. They lead with phrases like, "Tell me about your thinking…" "Please give a rationale for that perspective…" "Who agrees with that train of thought?" "I can hear that you are concerned about…" These strategies foster genuine interest in the viewpoints of each group member. It is important that each member feel heard, all the while realizing that the group think is ultimately more important than self-think. The journey is truly as important as the culminated result.

Creating and adhering to norms are critical parts of the facilitation process. Recall some sample norms discussed previously. Consider starting with a short list of suggested ideas and then solicit input from the group. As you do, define the behaviors and hold people accountable to abiding by them. Write them down. Be sure your agreed upon norms are visible for all to see and easy for you and others to reference during a meeting.

If you are relatively new to the facilitation process, start small. Consider mediating groups in limited scope and size like family meetings, church groups, book clubs, or even friend misunderstandings. The more you practice strategies and questioning tactics, the more competent and confident you become. Gather a variety of group processes to expand conversations and work toward agreement. Note a variety of protocols shared in the last book of this series.

To enhance your facilitation practices, consider having a process observer. This may be a trusted friend or colleague. They watch you as you facilitate a group and provide procedural feedback. Some questions for consideration might include:

- Were you able to treat all participants fairly and equally?

- Did you acknowledge all contributions similarly?

- Were you able to stay on topic?

- Did you catch the group when the group goes off topic and tell them?

- Were you able to avoid alignment to one side or position? Watch your comments to avoid giving any member of the group the impression that you have a closer relationship or more agreement with any group members.

- Were you able to involve participants by focusing on engaging participation, rather than evaluating the quality of the ideas being generated?

- Were you also able to stand strong, even in the face of conflict within the group.

- Were you also able to maintain neutrality and avoid judging any person or idea in conflict? Participants need to know that you are listening and not taking sides.

Adept facilitators help groups accomplish better and more thoughtful results than those often done independently. As Hunter, (2007) said, "Facilitators are called upon to fill an impartial role in helping groups to become more effective. We act as process guides to create a balance between participation and results" (p. 150). Mastering questioning strategies, processes and protocols, and being mindful of the inclusiveness trusted observers may offer, are ways to enhance your facilitator skills.

The Speaker's Toolkit

Seasoned speakers have learned many things, often the hard way. Each one has likely forgotten an important tool needed to make for a great presentation. Therefore, create a speaker's "toolkit" of resources and paraphernalia you might need onsite. For example, the following might be a useful checklist for you as you create your own toolkit.

- Power cord
- Hard drive with your presentation backed up
- Dongle or other converting device(s) for both VGA and HDMI projectors
- Clicker
- Microphone connectors (as needed)
- Internet hotspot
- Notecards

- Sticky notes
- Batteries (9 volt, AA, AAA) to use in clickers or microphones
- Tissues
- Lip balm
- Reading glasses (as needed)

Consider anything you will need to effectively facilitate an activity you are using. Never assume you will have technology support to assist you, so learn about connectors, power sources, and sound boards. Be prepared. Additionally, always pack your own resources, and refrain from informal discussions upon ending your presentation until your supplies are packed. Use the common refrain, "A place for everything and everything in its place" (Franklin, B. 1706).

Throughout part III, I highlighted important considerations for a dynamic delivery. Here I concentrated on the various considerations for delivering your message more dynamically. These included getting your group's

attention, using your voice effectively, minding presenter

behaviors, considerations for engagement, effective visual

enhancements, strategies for solid webinars and facilitated

sessions, as well as the all-important speaker's toolkit.

Strong presentation delivery is arduous. Yet, delivering

your message dynamically is a difference-maker.

Success is no accident. It is hard work, perseverance, learning, studying, sacrifice and most of all, love of what you are doing or learning to do.
Pele

Conclusion

This book is intended to help you make your message one that is remembered. Part one described important considerations for setting the stage—things like room arrangement, use of sound, managing the audience, and centering yourself. These suggestions help novice and expert presenters reflect about everything surrounding you and your messaging. Part two embodied essential elements for three types of introductions: informal, formal, and topic-based. Part three focused on a surplus of considerations for a delivering your message dynamically. Some ideas noted were getting your group's attention, using your voice effectively, presenter behaviors, engagement, visual enhancements, webinars, and the all-important speaker's toolkit. My hope is this series will assist you from your planning and preparation, to delivery, professionalism, and reflection. Go be better tomorrow than you were today!

References:

Allen, R., (2008). *Train smart: effective trainings every time* [second edition]. Thousand Oaks, CA: Corwin Press.

Bell, Christopher's conference presentation, freshmen orientation, UCCS: August 16, 2018.

Benjamin Franklin, Brainy Quote:
https://www.brainyquote.com/quotes/benjamin_franklin_109062

Blairy, Hilary's conference presentation "ARTiculate Real&Clear" Colorado National Speaker's Association conference November 1, 2018.

Bowman, S.L, (2009). *Training from the back of the room*. San Francisco, CA: John Wiley & Sons.

DiResta, D., (2019). *Knockout presentations: how to deliver your message with power, punch, and pizzaz*. [Kindle DX version]. Retrieved from amazon.com

Duarte, N., (2012). *HBR guide to persuasive presentations*. Boston, MA: Harvard Business School Publishing.

Eggert, M., (2010). *Brilliant body language*. Great Britain: Pearson.

Feinstein, S., (2006). *The Praeger handbook of learning and the brain* (volume 2). Westport, CT: Praeger Publishers.

Heflebower, T. (2018). *Presenting perfected: planning & preparing your message*. San Bernardino, CA: Amazon.

Hunter, D., (2007). *The art of facilitation* [revised edition]. San Francisco, CA: Jossey-Bass.

Gladwell, M:
https://www.brainyquote.com/quotes/malcolm_gladwell_395749?src=t_first_impressions

Gordon, P. (2010). Personal communication.

Jensen, E., (1998). *Trainer's bonanza: over 1000 fabulous tips & tools*. San Diego, CA: The Brain Store, Inc.

George Jessel:
https://www.brainyquote.com/quotes/george_jessel_392909

Karia, A., (2012). *How to deliver a great TED talk*. Akash Karia.
Kearsley, 2010

Martin, S., (2007). *Born standing up*. New York: NY. Scribner.

Pele (Edson Arantes Do Nascimento):
Read more at: https://www.brainyquote.com/quotes/pele_737774

Pike, B. (2003). Creative training techniques handbook (2ᵈ ed.). Minneapolis: Lakewood Books.

Reynolds, G., (2010). *Presentationzen* design: simple design principles and techniques to enhance your presentations. Berkeley, CA: New Riders.

Solem, L., & Pike, B, (1997). *50 creative training closers*. San Francisco, CA: Jossey-Bass Pfeiffer.

Michael R. Solomon, Gokcen Coskuner and Caroline Lego Muñoz (2005), "You are What You Wear: Fashion as Social Process," in ed. Tulio Gregory, Fashion Encyclopedia, Rome: Istituto della Enciclopedia Italiana.

Strengthening your communication skills with clients. https://blog.nasm.org/newletter/strengthening-communication-skills-clients/ February 20, 2015. Fitness professionals newsletter.

Biography

Tammy Heflebower, Ed.D., is a highly sought-after presenter and consultant with vast experiences in urban, rural, and suburban communities throughout The United States, Australia, Canada, Denmark, Great Britain, and The Netherlands. Dr. Heflebower has served as an award-winning classroom teacher, building and district educational leader, regional professional development director, national and international trainer, and leadership consultant. Tammy was also an adjunct professor at several universities, and a prominent member and leader of numerous statewide and national organizations.

Dr. Heflebower was the vice president and then senior scholar at Marzano Research prior to becoming the CEO of her own company, !nspire Inc: Education and Business Solutions.

Dr. Heflebower widely published. She is an award-winning author and coauthor of over a dozen books and articles focusing on organizational and educational leadership and teambuilding. She also specializes in powerful presentation and facilitation techniques, and is sole author of the *Presenting Perfected* book series.

Tammy holds a bachelor of arts from Hastings College in Hastings, Nebraska, where she was honored as an *Outstanding Young Alumna* and the team of which she was a part, was inducted into the athletic hall of fame. She has a master of arts from the University of Nebraska–Omaha and an educational administrative endorsement from the University of Nebraska–Lincoln. She also earned a doctor of education in educational administration from the University of Nebraska–Lincoln.

Dr. Heflebower regularly works with business and educational entities on site, and she regularly presents at national and international conferences. She provides keynote coaching, facilitation, presenter training, and one-one coaching. Contact Dr. Heflebower from her website at: www.inspirementor.com, by email at: tammyheflebower@gmail.com and follow her on twitter @tammyhef.

Acknowledgements

I want to thank all those wonderful teachers and presenters from whom I've learned. Kathy Woodward, Dave Rosenbaum, and Jan Watkins, you were teachers who made such a difference in my life! You taught me when you didn't even realize it. A special thanks to Robert Marzano for giving me the platform to hone my craft and use my skills. You have mentored me and helped my see and use my gift of inspiration.

To all of my family and dear friends, thank you for your unending belief in me and your amazing support. A distinctive thanks for my friends and colleagues Jan Hoegh and Phil Warrick. You have served as life-long friends and teammates like no others! You drive me to be my best, everyday! Thanks to all who challenged me to live my dreams.

www.ingramcontent.com/pod-product-compliance
Lightning Source LLC
Chambersburg PA
CBHW020926180526
45163CB00007B/2903